THE COMPLETE GUIDE TO WEB DEVELOPMENT WITH React AND Node.js

Techniques for Fast, Scalable, and Secure Apps

CONTENTS

GETTING STARTED WITH REACT AND NODEJS

Introduction to React

React is a popular JavaScript library for building user interfaces, particularly single-page applications. It was developed by Facebook and has gained widespread adoption due to its efficiency and flexibility.

Key concepts in React:

1. Components: React applications are built using components, which are reusable pieces of UI.

2. Virtual DOM: React uses a virtual representation of the DOM for efficient updates.

3. Unidirectional data flow: Data in React flows in one direction, making applications easier to understand and debug.

Let's look at a simple React component:

```jsx
import React from 'react';
function Welcome(props) {
  return <h1>Hello, {props.name}!</h1>;
}
export default Welcome;
```

This component takes a `name` prop and renders a greeting. We can use it like this:

```jsx
import React from 'react';
import Welcome from './Welcome';
function App() {
  return (
    <div>
      <Welcome name="Alice" />
      <Welcome name="Bob" />
    </div>
  );
}
export default App;
```

Setting up a Node.js environment

Node.js is a JavaScript runtime built on Chrome's V8 JavaScript engine. It allows you to run JavaScript on the server-side and is often used to build backend services for web applications.

To set up a Node.js environment:

1. Download and install Node.js from the official website (https://nodejs.org/).

2. Verify the installation by opening a terminal and running:

```bash
node --version
npm --version
```

These commands should display the versions of Node.js and npm (Node Package Manager) installed on your system.

3. Create a new directory for your project and initialize it with npm:

```bash

mkdir my-react-node-project
cd my-react-node-project
npm init -y
```

This creates a `package.json` file, which will manage your project's dependencies.

Creating your first React-Node.js project

Now that we have Node.js set up, let's create a simple React application using Create React App, and then add a basic Node.js backend.

First, let's create the React frontend:

```Bash
npx create-react-app frontend
cd frontend
npm start"
```

This will create a new React application and start a development server. You should see the default React app running at http://localhost:3000.

Now, let's create a simple Node.js backend. In the root of your project directory:

```bash
mkdir backend
cd backend
npm init -y

npm install express
```

Create a file named `server.js` in the backend directory:

```javascript
const express = require('express');
const app = express();
const port = 5000;

app.get('/api/hello', (req, res) => {
  res.json({ message: 'Hello from the backend!' });
});

app.listen(port, () => {
  console.log(`Backend server running on port
${port}`);
});
```

This creates a simple Express server with one route that returns a JSON response.

To run the backend server:

```bash
node server.js
```

Now you have a React frontend and a Node.js backend running simultaneously. To connect them, you'll need to set up a proxy in your React app. Add this line to your frontend's `package.json`:

```json
"proxy": "http://localhost:5000"
```

This allows the frontend to make requests to the backend without specifying the full URL.

Understanding JSX and component basics

JSX is a syntax extension for JavaScript that looks similar to XML or HTML. It allows you to write HTML-like code in your JavaScript files, which is then transformed into regular JavaScript by tools like Babel.

Here's an example of JSX:

```jsx
const element = <h1>Hello, world!</h1>;
```

This might look like HTML, but it's actually JavaScript. When compiled, it turns into:

```javascript
const element = React.createElement('h1', null, 'Hello, world!');
```

JSX makes it easier to write and understand the structure of React components.

Let's create a more complex component to demonstrate JSX and component basics:

```jsx
import React, { useState } from 'react';
```

```
function Counter() {
  const [count, setCount] = useState(0);
  return (
    <div>
      <p>You clicked {count} times</p>
      <button onClick={() => setCount(count + 1)}>
        Click me
      </button>
    </div>
  );
}

export default Counter;
```

This component demonstrates several important React concepts:

1. Hooks: We're using the `useState` hook to add state to our functional component.

2. JSX: The component's structure is written in JSX, which allows us to mix JavaScript expressions (like `{count}`) with HTML-like syntax.

3. Event handling: We're using the `onClick` prop to handle button clicks.

To use this component in your app, you would import it and render it like this:

```jsx
import React from 'react';
import Counter from './Counter';
function App() {
  return (
    <div>
      <h1>Welcome to my app</h1>
      <Counter />
    </div>
  );
}
export default App;
```

Now let's create a more complex example that combines React on the frontend with our Node.js backend. We'll create a simple todo list application.

First, update your backend `server.js`:

```javascript
const express = require('express');
const app = express();
const port = 5000;
app.use(express.json());
let todos = [
  {id: 1, text: 'Learn React', completed: false },
  {id: 2, text: 'Build a React-Node.js app', completed:
false }
```

```javascript
];
app.get('/api/todos', (req, res) => {
  res.json(todos);
});

app.post('/api/todos', (req, res) => {
  const newTodo = {
    id: todos.length + 1,

text: req.body.text,
    completed: false
  };
  todos.push(newTodo);
  res.status(201).json(newTodo);
});
app.put('/api/todos/:id', (req, res) => {
  const id = parseInt(req.params.id);
  const todo = todos.find(t => t.id === id);
  if (todo) {
    todo.completed = req.body.completed;
    res.json(todo);
  } else {
    res.status(404).json({ error: 'Todo not found' });
  }
});
app.listen(port, () => {
  console.log(`Backend server running on port
${port}`);
});
```

Now, let's create a React component to display and interact with our todos. Create a new file called `TodoList.js` in your frontend's `src` directory:

```jsx
import React, {useState, useEffect} from 'react';
function TodoList() {
  const [todos, setTodos] = useState([]);
  const [newTodo, setNewTodo] = useState('');
  useEffect(() => {
    fetchTodos();
  }, []);
  const fetchTodos = async () => {
    const response = await fetch('/api/todos');
    const data = await response.json();
    setTodos(data);
  };
  const addTodo = async (e) => {
    e.preventDefault();
    const response = await fetch('/api/todos', {
      method: 'POST',
      headers: {'Content-Type': 'application/json' },
      body: JSON.stringify({ text: newTodo })
    });
    const todo = await response.json();
    setTodos([...todos, todo]);
    setNewTodo('');
  };
```

```
const toggleTodo = async (id) => {
  const todo = todos.find(t => t.id === id);
  const response = await fetch(`/api/todos/${id}`, {
    method: 'PUT',
    headers: { 'Content-Type': 'application/json' },
    body: JSON.stringify({ completed: !todo.completed
})
  });
  const updatedTodo = await response.json();
  setTodos(todos.map(t => t.id === id ? updatedTodo :
t));
};
return (
  <div>
    <h1>Todo List</h1>
    <form onSubmit={addTodo}>
      <input
        type="text"
        value={newTodo}
        onChange={(e) => setNewTodo(e.target.value)}
        placeholder="Add a new todo"
      />
      <button type="submit">Add</button>
    </form>
    <ul>
      {todos.map(todo => (
        <li key={todo.id} onClick={() =>
toggleTodo(todo.id)} style={{ textDecoration:
todo.completed ? 'line-through' : 'none' }}>
```

```
            {todo.text}
          </li>
        ))}
      </ul>
    </div>
  );
}
export default TodoList;
```

This component demonstrates several important concepts:

1. State management: We're using the `useState` hook to manage the list of todos and the new todo input.

2. Side effects: We're using the `useEffect` hook to fetch todos when the component mounts.

3. Event handling: We're handling form submission and todo item clicks.

4. Rendering lists: We're using the `map` function to render the list of todos.

5. Conditional styling: We're applying a style based on whether a todo is completed.

To use this component, update your `App.js`:

```jsx
import React from 'react';
import TodoList from './TodoList';
```

```
function App() {
  return (
    <div className="App">
      <TodoList />
    </div>
  );
}
export default App;
```

Now you have a full-stack application with a React frontend and a Node.js backend! The frontend allows users to view, add, and toggle todos, while the backend handles data persistence and API requests.

This example demonstrates how React and Node.js can work together to create interactive web applications. React handles the user interface and state management on the client-side, while Node.js provides a server for handling API requests and data storage.

As you continue to develop your skills, you'll learn more advanced techniques like state management with Redux, authentication, database integration, and deployment strategies. But this foundation gives you a solid start in building applications with React and Node.js.

Remember to always consult the official documentation for React and Node.js as you develop your projects, as they provide the most up-to-date and comprehensive information on these technologies.

BUILDING THE FRONTEND WITH REACT

React Components and Props

React applications are built using components, which are reusable pieces of UI. Components can be either function components or class components. In modern React development, function components are preferred due to their simplicity and the introduction of hooks.

Let's start with a simple function component:

```jsx
function Greeting(props) {
  return <h1>Hello, { props.name }!</h1>;
}
```

This component takes a `name` prop and renders a greeting. We can use it like this:

```jsx
<Greeting name="Alice" />
```

Props are read-only and help make your components reusable. You can pass any JavaScript value as a prop, including objects, arrays, and functions.

Let's create a more complex component that demonstrates the use of multiple props:

```jsx
function UserProfile(props) {
  return (
    <div className="user-profile">
      <img src={props.avatarUrl} alt={props.name} />
      <h2>{props.name}</h2>
      <p>Age: {props.age}</p>
      <p>Occupation: {props.occupation}</p>
    </div>
  );
}
```

We can use this component like this:

```jsx
<UserProfile
  name="Alice Johnson"
  age= {28}
  occupation="Software Developer"
  avatarUrl="https://example.com/avatar.jpg"
/>
```

You can also use object destructuring to make your component more readable:

```jsx
function UserProfile({ name, age, occupation, avatarUrl
}) {
  return (
    <div className="user-profile">
      <img src={avatarUrl} alt={name} />
      <h2>{name}</h2>
      <p>Age: {age}</p>
      <p>Occupation: {occupation}</p>
    </div>
  );
}
```

State Management and Hooks

State in React refers to data that can change over time. When state changes, React re-renders the component to reflect these changes.

The `useState` hook is used to add state to function components. Here's an example:

```jsx
import React, { useState } from 'react';
function Counter() {
  const [count, setCount] = useState(0);
  return (
    <div>
      <p>You clicked {count} times</p>
      <button onClick={() => setCount(count + 1)}>
```

```jsx
        Click me
      </button>
    </div>
  );
}
```

In this example, `useState` returns an array with two elements: the current state value and a function to update it. We use array destructuring to assign these to `count` and `setCount`.

Another important hook is `useEffect`, which lets you perform side effects in function components:

```jsx
jsx

import React, { useState, useEffect } from 'react';
function DataFetcher() {
  const [data, setData] = useState(null);
  useEffect(() => {
    fetch('https://api.example.com/data')
      .then(response => response.json())
      .then(data => setData(data));
  }, []); // Empty dependency array means this effect
runs once on mount
  if (data === null) {
    return <div>Loading...</div>;
  }
  return <div> { JSON.stringify(data) } </div>;
}
```

This component fetches data when it mounts and updates the state when the data is received.

For more complex state management, you might consider using the Context API or a state management library like Redux. Here's a simple example using the Context API:

```jsx
import React, { createContext, useContext, useState }
from 'react';
const ThemeContext = createContext();
function ThemeProvider({ children }) {
  const [theme, setTheme] = useState('light');

  return (
    <ThemeContext.Provider value= {{ theme, setTheme
}}>
      { children }
    </ThemeContext.Provider>
  );
}
function ThemedButton() {
  const { theme, setTheme } = useContext(ThemeContext);
  return (
    <button
      onClick={() => setTheme(theme === 'light' ?
'dark' : 'light')}
      style={{
```

```
        background: theme === 'light' ? '#fff' :
'#000',
        color: theme === 'light' ? '#000' : '#fff',
      }}
    >
      Toggle Theme
    </button>
  );
}
function App() {
  return (
    <ThemeProvider>
      <div>
        <h1>Themed App</h1>
        <ThemedButton />
      </div>
    </ThemeProvider>
  );
}
```

Routing with React Router

React Router is a popular library for handling routing in React applications. It allows you to create a single-page application with navigation without the page refreshing as the user navigates.

First, install React Router:

```bash
npm install react-router-dom
```

Here's a basic example of how to use React Router:

```jsx
import React from 'react';
import {BrowserRouter as Router, Route, Link, Switch}
from 'react-router-dom';
function Home() {
  return <h2>Home Page</h2>;
}
function About() {
  return <h2>About Page</h2>;
}

function Users() {
  return <h2>Users Page</h2>;
}
function App() {
```

```
return (
  <Router>
    <div>
      <nav>
        <ul>
          <li>
            <Link to="/">Home</Link>
          </li>
          <li>
            <Link to="/about">About</Link>
          </li>
          <li>
            <Link to="/users">Users</Link>
          </li>
        </ul>
      </nav>
      <Switch>
        <Route path="/about">
          <About />
        </Route>
        <Route path="/users">
          <Users />
        </Route>
        <Route path="/">
          <Home />
        </Route>
      </Switch>
    </div>
  </Router>
```

```
  );
}
```

This sets up a basic routing structure with three pages. The `Link` component is used for navigation, and the `Route` component renders the appropriate component based on the current URL.

You can also use dynamic routing with URL parameters:

```jsx
import React from 'react';
import { BrowserRouter as Router, Route, Link, Switch,
useParams } from 'react-router-dom';
function User() {
  let { id } = useParams();
  return <h2>User: {id}</h2>;
}
function App() {
  return (
    <Router>
      <div>
        <nav>
          <ul>
            <li>
              <Link to="/user/1">User 1</Link>
            </li>
            <li>
              <Link to="/user/2">User 2</Link>
            </li>
```

```jsx
      </ul>
    </nav>
    <Switch>
      <Route path="/user/:id">
        <User />
      </Route>
    </Switch>
  </div>
</Router>
  );
}
```

Forms and User Input Handling

Handling forms in React involves using state to control the form inputs. Here's an example of a controlled component:

```jsx
import React, { useState } from 'react';
function NameForm() {
  const [name, setName] = useState('');
  const handleSubmit = (event) => {
    event.preventDefault();
    alert('A name was submitted: ' + name);
  }
  return (
    <form onSubmit={handleSubmit}>
      <label>
```

```jsx
      Name:
      <input
        type="text"
        value={name}
        onChange={(e) => setName(e.target.value)}
      />
    </label>
    <input type="submit" value="Submit" />
  </form>
  );
}
```

In this example, the `name` state controls the value of the input. When the user types, the `onChange` event updates the state, which in turn updates the input value.

For more complex forms, you might want to use a library like Formik. Here's a basic example:

```jsx
import React from 'react';
import { Formik, Form, Field, ErrorMessage } from
'formik';
function ValidatedForm() {
  return (
    <Formik
      initialValues={{ email: '', password: '' }}
      validate={values => {
        const errors = {};
```

```
        if (!values.email) {
          errors.email = 'Required';
        } else if (
          !/^[A-Z0-9._%+-]+@[A-Z0-9.-]+\.[A-
Z]{2,}$/i.test(values.email)
        ) {
          errors.email = 'Invalid email address';
        }
        return errors;
      }}
      onSubmit={(values, { setSubmitting }) => {
        setTimeout(() => {
          alert(JSON.stringify(values, null, 2));
          setSubmitting(false);
        }, 400);
      }}
    >
      {({ isSubmitting }) => (
        <Form>
          <Field type="email" name="email" />
          <ErrorMessage name="email" component="div" />
          <Field type="password" name="password" />
          <ErrorMessage name="password" component="div"
/>
          <button type="submit"
disabled={isSubmitting}>
            Submit
          </button>
        </Form>
```

```
    )}
  </Formik>
  );
}
```

This form includes validation and handles form submission.

Optimizing Performance with React

React is generally fast out of the box, but there are several techniques you can use to optimize performance:

1. **Use the Production Build:** Always use the production build of React in production. It's significantly faster than the development build.

2. **Virtualization for Long Lists:** If you're rendering long lists, consider using a library like `react-window` to only render the items that are currently visible:

```jsx
import React from 'react';
import { FixedSizeList as List } from 'react-window';
function Row({ index, style }) {
  return <div style={style}>Row {index}</div>;
}
function LongList() {
```

```
  return (
    <List
      height={400}
      itemCount={1000}
      itemSize={35}
      width={300}
    >
      {Row}
    </List>
  );
}
```

3. **Memoization:** Use React.memo for function components that render often with the same props:

```jsx
import React from 'react';
const MyComponent = React.memo(function
MyComponent(props) {
  /* render using props */
});
```

4. **Use useCallback for Event Handlers:** If you're passing callbacks to optimized child components, you can prevent unnecessary re-renders by using `useCallback`:

```jsx
import React, { useState, useCallback } from 'react';
function Parent() {
  const [count, setCount] = useState(0);
  const increment = useCallback(() => {
    setCount(c => c + 1);
  }, []);
  return <Child onIncrement={increment} />;
}
const Child = React.memo(({ onIncrement }) => {
  console.log('Child rendered');
  return <button
onClick={onIncrement}>Increment</button>;
});
```

5. Lazy Loading with Suspense: For larger applications, you can use lazy loading to split your code into smaller chunks and load components only when they're needed:

```jsx
import React, { Suspense, lazy } from 'react';
import { BrowserRouter as Router, Route, Switch } from
'react-router-dom';
const Home = lazy(() => import('./routes/Home'));
const About = lazy(() => import('./routes/About'));
function App() {
  return (
    <Router>
```

```jsx
      <Suspense fallback={<div>Loading...</div>}>
        <Switch>
          <Route exact path="/" component={Home}/>
          <Route path="/about" component={About}/>
        </Switch>
      </Suspense>
    </Router>
  );
}
```

6. **Use the useReducer Hook for Complex State Logic:** For components with complex state logic, `useReducer` may be more appropriate than `useState`:

```jsx
jsx

import React, { useReducer } from 'react';
function reducer(state, action) {
  switch (action.type) {
    case 'increment':
      return {count: state.count + 1};
    case 'decrement':
      return {count: state.count - 1};
    default:
      throw new Error();
  }
}
function Counter() {
```

```
  const [state, dispatch] = useReducer(reducer, {
count: 0 });
  return (
    <>
      Count: {state.count}
      <button onClick={() => dispatch({type:
'decrement'})}>-</button>
      <button onClick={() => dispatch({type:
'increment'})}>+</button>
    </>
  );
}
```

These techniques can significantly improve the performance of your React applications, especially as they grow in size and complexity. Remember, premature optimization is the root of all evil – only optimize when you have a measurable performance problem.

In conclusion, building the frontend with React involves understanding components and props, managing state effectively, implementing routing for navigation, handling forms and user input, and optimizing performance. By mastering these concepts and techniques, you'll be well-equipped to build robust, efficient, and user-friendly web applications with React.

Remember to always refer to the official React documentation for the most up-to-date information and best practices. As you continue to develop your skills, you'll discover even more advanced techniques and patterns for building complex applications with React.

DEVELOPING THE BACKEND WITH NODE.JS AND EXPRESS

Setting up an Express server

Express is a minimal and flexible Node.js web application framework that provides a robust set of features for web and mobile applications. Let's start by setting up a basic Express server.

First, initialize a new Node.js project and install Express:

```bash
bash

mkdir express-server
cd express-server
npm init -y
npm install express
```

Now, create a file named `server.js` and add the following code:

```javascript
javascript

const express = require('express');
const app = express();
const port = 3000;
app.get('/', (req, res) => {
  res.send('Hello World!');
});

app.listen(port, () => {
```

```
    console.log(`Server running at
http://localhost:${port}`);
});
```

This creates a simple Express server that responds with "Hello World!" when you visit the root URL. To run the server:

```bash
node server.js
```

Let's expand this to include some basic routing:

```javascript
const express = require('express');
const app = express();
const port = 3000;
app.use(express.json()); // Middleware to parse JSON
bodies
app.get('/', (req, res) => {
  res.send('Hello World!');
});
app.get('/api/users', (req, res) => {
  // In a real app, this would fetch from a database
  const users = [
    { id: 1, name: 'Alice' },
    { id: 2, name: 'Bob' }
  ];
  res.json(users);
```

```
});
app.post('/api/users', (req, res) => {
  // In a real app, this would add to a database
  console.log('Received new user:', req.body);
  res.status(201).json({ message: 'User created' });
});
app.listen(port, () => {
  console.log(`Server running at
http://localhost:${port}`);
});
```

This server now has two routes: a GET route to fetch users and a POST route to create a new user.

RESTful API design principles

REST (Representational State Transfer) is an architectural style for designing networked applications. RESTful APIs typically use HTTP methods explicitly and have a consistent URL structure. Here are some key principles:

1. Use HTTP methods correctly:

   - GET: Retrieve a resource

   - POST: Create a new resource

   - PUT: Update an existing resource

   - DELETE: Delete a resource

2. Use nouns instead of verbs in endpoint paths

3. Use logical nesting on endpoints

4. Handle errors gracefully and return standard error codes

5. Allow filtering, sorting, and pagination

6. Versioning your API

Let's implement a RESTful API for a simple blog application:

```javascript
const express = require('express');
const app = express();
const port = 3000;
app.use(express.json());
let posts = [
  { id: 1, title: 'First post', content: 'Hello world!'
},
  { id: 2, title: 'Second post', content: 'Another
post.' }
];

// Get all posts
app.get('/api/posts', (req, res) => {
  res.json(posts);
});

// Get a specific post
app.get('/api/posts/:id', (req, res) => {
```

```javascript
  const post = posts.find(p => p.id ===
parseInt(req.params.id));
  if (!post) return res.status(404).json({ message:
'Post not found' });
  res.json(post);
});

// Create a new post
app.post('/api/posts', (req, res) => {
  const post = {
    id: posts.length + 1,
    title: req.body.title,
    content: req.body.content
  };
  posts.push(post);
  res.status(201).json(post);
});

// Update a post
app.put('/api/posts/:id', (req, res) => {
  const post = posts.find(p => p.id ===
parseInt(req.params.id));
  if (!post) return res.status(404).json({ message:
'Post not found' });

  post.title = req.body.title;
  post.content = req.body.content;
  res.json(post);
});
```

```
// Delete a post
app.delete('/api/posts/:id', (req, res) => {
  const postIndex = posts.findIndex(p => p.id ===
parseInt(req.params.id));
  if (postIndex === -1) return res.status(404).json({
message: 'Post not found' });

  posts.splice(postIndex, 1);
  res.status(204).end();
});

app.listen(port, () => {
  console.log(`Server running at
http://localhost:${port}`);
});
```

This API follows RESTful principles:

- It uses appropriate HTTP methods for different operations.

- The endpoints use nouns (posts) instead of verbs.

- It returns appropriate status codes (201 for creation, 404 for not found, etc.).

Middleware and error handling

Middleware functions are functions that have access to the request object (req), the response object (res), and the next middleware function in the application's request-response cycle, usually denoted by a variable named `next`.

Let's add some middleware to our application:

```javascript
const express = require('express');
const app = express();
// Middleware for logging
app.use((req, res, next) => {
  console.log(`${new Date().toISOString()} -
${req.method} ${req.url}`);
  next();
});

// Middleware for parsing JSON bodies
app.use(express.json());

// Middleware for setting headers
app.use((req, res, next) => {
  res.setHeader('X-Powered-By', 'Your App Name');
  next();
});

// Error handling middleware
app.use((err, req, res, next) => {
  console.error(err.stack);
  res.status(500).json({ message: 'Something went
wrong!' });
```

```
});

// Your routes go here

app.listen(3000, () => console.log('Server started'));
"
```

For more specific error handling, you can create custom error classes:

```javascript
class NotFoundError extends Error {
  constructor(message) {
    super(message);
    this.name = 'NotFoundError';
    this.statusCode = 404;
  }
}
app.get('/api/posts/:id', (req, res, next) => {
  const post = posts.find(p => p.id ===
parseInt(req.params.id));
  if (!post) {
    next(new NotFoundError('Post not found'));
  } else {
    res.json(post);
  }
});
app.use((err, req, res, next) => {
  if (err instanceof NotFoundError) {
    res.status(err.statusCode).json({ message:
err.message });
```

```
  } else {
    console.error(err.stack);
    res.status(500).json({ message: 'Something went
wrong!' });
  }
});
```

Database integration (MongoDB and SQL options)

Let's look at integrating both MongoDB (a NoSQL database) and MySQL (a SQL database) with our Express application.

First, for MongoDB using Mongoose:

```bash
bash

npm install mongoose
```

```javascript
javascript

const mongoose = require('mongoose');
const express = require('express');
const app = express();

mongoose.connect('mongodb://localhost/myblog', {
useNewUrlParser: true, useUnifiedTopology: true });

const PostSchema = new mongoose.Schema({
  title: String,
  content: String,
  createdAt: { type: Date, default: Date.now }
});

const Post = mongoose.model('Post', PostSchema);

app.use(express.json());
```

```javascript
app.get('/api/posts', async (req, res) => {
  const posts = await Post.find();
  res.json(posts);
});

app.post('/api/posts', async (req, res) => {
  const post = new Post({
    title: req.body.title,
    content: req.body.content
  });
  await post.save();
  res.status(201).json(post);
});

app.listen(3000, () => console.log('Server started'));
```

Now, for MySQL using the `mysql2` package:

```bash
bash

npm install mysql2
```

```javascript
javascript

const mysql = require('mysql2/promise');
const express = require('express');
const app = express();
const pool = mysql.createPool({
  host: 'localhost',
```

```
    user: 'your_username',
    password: 'your_password',
    database: 'myblog',
    waitForConnections: true,
    connectionLimit: 10,
    queueLimit: 0
});
app.use(express.json());
app.get('/api/posts', async (req, res) => {
  const [rows] = await pool.query('SELECT * FROM
posts');
  res.json(rows);
});
app.post('/api/posts', async (req, res) => {
  const { title, content } = req.body;
  const [result] = await pool.query(
    'INSERT INTO posts (title, content) VALUES (?, ?)',
    [title, content]
  );
  res.status(201).json({ id: result.insertId, title,
content });
});
app.listen(3000, () => console.log('Server started'));
```

Authentication and authorization

Authentication verifies who a user is, while authorization
determines what they're allowed to do. Let's implement a simple
JWT (JSON Web Token) based authentication system:

First, install required packages:

```bash
npm install bcryptjs jsonwebtoken
```

Now, let's create a simple authentication system:

```javascript
const express = require('express');
const bcrypt = require('bcryptjs');
const jwt = require('jsonwebtoken');
const app = express();

app.use(express.json());

// In a real app, you'd store users in a database
let users = [];

const SECRET_KEY = 'your-secret-key'; // In a real app,
use an environment variable

app.post('/api/register', async (req, res) => {
  const { username, password } = req.body;

  // Check if user already exists
  if (users.find(u => u.username === username)) {
```

```
    return res.status(400).json({ message: 'User
already exists' });
  }

  // Hash password
  const hashedPassword = await bcrypt.hash(password,
10);

  // Save user
  users.push({ username, password: hashedPassword });

  res.status(201).json({ message: 'User created
successfully' });
});

app.post('/api/login', async (req, res) => {
  const { username, password } = req.body;

  // Find user
  const user = users.find(u => u.username ===
username);
  if (!user) {
    return res.status(400).json({ message: 'User not
found' });
  }

  // Check password
  const validPassword = await bcrypt.compare(password,
user.password);
```

```
  if (!validPassword) {
     return res.status(400).json({ message: 'Invalid
password' });
  }

  // Create and assign token
  const token = jwt.sign({ username: user.username },
SECRET_KEY, { expiresIn: '1h' });
  res.json({ token });
});

// Middleware to verify token
function authenticateToken(req, res, next) {
  const authHeader = req.headers['authorization'];
  const token = authHeader && authHeader.split(' ')[1];

  if (token == null) return res.sendStatus(401);

  jwt.verify(token, SECRET_KEY, (err, user) => {
    if (err) return res.sendStatus(403);
    req.user = user;
    next();
  });
}

// Protected route
app.get('/api/protected', authenticateToken, (req, res)
=> {
```

```javascript
      res.json({ message: 'This is a protected route',
user: req.user });
});


app.listen(3000, () => console.log('Server started'));
```

This setup provides basic authentication and authorization:

1. Users can register with a username and password.

2. Passwords are hashed before being stored.

3. Users can log in and receive a JWT.

4. The JWT can be used to access protected routes.

For more complex authorization, you might want to implement role-based access control (RBAC):

```javascript
javascript

const ROLES = {
  ADMIN: 'admin',
  USER: 'user'
};


// Middleware to check role
function checkRole(role) {
  return (req, res, next) => {
    if (req.user.role !== role) {
      res.status(403).json({ message: 'Access denied'
});
```

```
    } else {
      next();
    }
  }
}
// Admin-only route
app.get('/api/admin', authenticateToken,
checkRole(ROLES.ADMIN), (req, res) => {
  res.json({ message: 'This is an admin-only route' });
});
```

In conclusion, developing a backend with Node.js and Express involves setting up a server, designing RESTful APIs, implementing middleware for various tasks including error handling, integrating with databases, and implementing authentication and authorization.

Remember to always follow security best practices:

1. Never store passwords in plain text.

2. Use HTTPS in production.

3. Implement rate limiting to prevent brute-force attacks.

4. Keep your dependencies up to date.

5. Validate and sanitize all user inputs.

As you continue to develop your backend skills, you'll encounter more advanced topics like caching, microservices architecture, and automated testing. Always refer to the official documentation for Express, Node.js, and any libraries you use for the most up-to-date information and best practices.

FULL-STACK INTEGRATION AND DATA FLOW

Connecting React frontend to Node.js backend

When connecting a React frontend to a Node.js backend, we typically use HTTP requests to communicate between the two. The most common approach is to use the Fetch API or a library like Axios to make these requests.

First, let's set up a simple Express backend:

```javascript
// server.js
const express = require('express');
const cors = require('cors');
const app = express();
const port = 5000;
app.use(cors());
app.use(express.json());
let todos = [
  { id: 1, text: 'Learn React', completed: false },
  { id: 2, text: 'Learn Node.js', completed: false }
];
app.get('/api/todos', (req, res) => {
  res.json(todos);
});
app.post('/api/todos', (req, res) => {
  const newTodo = {
```

```
    id: todos.length + 1,
    text: req.body.text,
    completed: false
  };
  todos.push(newTodo);
  res.status(201).json(newTodo);
});

app.listen(port, () => {
  console.log(`Server running on port ${port}`);
});
```

Now, let's create a React component that interacts with this backend:

```jsx
// TodoList.js
import React, { useState, useEffect } from 'react';
function TodoList() {
  const [todos, setTodos] = useState([]);
  const [newTodo, setNewTodo] = useState('');
  useEffect(() => {
    fetchTodos();
  }, []);
  const fetchTodos = async () => {
    try {
      const response = await
fetch('http://localhost:5000/api/todos');
      const data = await response.json();
```

```
      setTodos(data);
    } catch (error) {
      console.error('Error fetching todos:', error);
    }
  };
  const addTodo = async (e) => {
    e.preventDefault();
    try {
      const response = await
fetch('http://localhost:5000/api/todos', {
        method: 'POST',
        headers: {
          'Content-Type': 'application/json',
        },
        body: JSON.stringify({ text: newTodo }),
      });
      const data = await response.json();
      setTodos([...todos, data]);
      setNewTodo('');
    } catch (error) {
      console.error('Error adding todo:', error);
    }
  };
  return (
    <div>
      <h1>Todo List</h1>
      <ul>
        {todos.map(todo => (
          <li key={todo.id}>{todo.text}</li>
```

```
      ))}
    </ul>
    <form onSubmit={addTodo}>
      <input
        type="text"
        value={newTodo}
        onChange={(e) => setNewTodo(e.target.value)}
        placeholder="Add new todo"
      />
      <button type="submit">Add Todo</button>
    </form>
  </div>
  );
}
export default TodoList;
```

This component fetches todos from the backend when it mounts and allows users to add new todos. The communication between frontend and backend is handled through HTTP requests.

State management with Redux or Context API

For more complex applications, we often need more robust state management solutions. Let's look at both Redux and the Context API.

First, Redux:

```bash
npm install redux react-redux @reduxjs/toolkit
```

"

```javascript
// store.js
import { configureStore, createSlice } from
'@reduxjs/toolkit';
const todoSlice = createSlice({
  name: 'todos',
  initialState: [],
  reducers: {
    setTodos: (state, action) => {
      return action.payload;
    },
    addTodo: (state, action) => {
      state.push(action.payload);
    },
  },
});

export const { setTodos, addTodo } = todoSlice.actions;

export const store = configureStore({
  reducer: {
    todos: todoSlice.reducer,
  },
});
```

```jsx
// App.js
import React from 'react';
import { Provider } from 'react-redux';
import { store } from './store';
import TodoList from './TodoList';

function App() {
  return (
    <Provider store={store}>
      <TodoList />
    </Provider>
  );
}

export default App;
```

```jsx
// TodoList.js
import React, { useState, useEffect } from 'react';
import { useSelector, useDispatch } from 'react-redux';
import { setTodos, addTodo } from './store';

function TodoList() {
  const todos = useSelector(state => state.todos);
  const dispatch = useDispatch();
  const [newTodo, setNewTodo] = useState('');
```

```
  useEffect(() => {
    fetchTodos();
  }, []);

  const fetchTodos = async () => {
    try {
      const response = await
fetch('http://localhost:5000/api/todos');
      const data = await response.json();
      dispatch(setTodos(data));
    } catch (error) {
      console.error('Error fetching todos:', error);
    }
  };

  const handleAddTodo = async (e) => {
    e.preventDefault();
    try {
      const response = await
fetch('http://localhost:5000/api/todos', {
        method: 'POST',
        headers: {
          'Content-Type': 'application/json',
        },
        body: JSON.stringify({ text: newTodo }),
      });
      const data = await response.json();
      dispatch(addTodo(data));
```

```
      setNewTodo('');
    } catch (error) {
      console.error('Error adding todo:', error);
    }
  };

  return (
    <div>
      <h1>Todo List</h1>
      <ul>
        {todos.map(todo => (
          <li key={todo.id}>{todo.text}</li>
        ))}
      </ul>
      <form onSubmit={handleAddTodo}>
        <input
          type="text"
          value={newTodo}
          onChange={(e) => setNewTodo(e.target.value)}
          placeholder="Add new todo"
        />
        <button type="submit">Add Todo</button>
      </form>
    </div>
  );
}
export default TodoList;
```

Now, let's look at the same example using the Context API:

```jsx

// TodoContext.js
import React, { createContext, useContext, useState }
from 'react';

const TodoContext = createContext();

export const useTodoContext = () =>
useContext(TodoContext);

export const TodoProvider = ({ children }) => {
  const [todos, setTodos] = useState([]);

  const addTodo = (todo) => {
    setTodos([...todos, todo]);
  };

  return (
    <TodoContext.Provider value={{ todos, setTodos,
addTodo }}>
      {children}
    </TodoContext.Provider>
  );
};
```

```jsx

// App.js
```

```jsx
import React from 'react';
import { TodoProvider } from './TodoContext';
import TodoList from './TodoList';

function App() {
  return (
    <TodoProvider>
      <TodoList />
    </TodoProvider>
  );
}

export default App;
```

jsx

```jsx
// TodoList.js
import React, { useState, useEffect } from 'react';
import { useTodoContext } from './TodoContext';

function TodoList() {
  const { todos, setTodos, addTodo } =
useTodoContext();
  const [newTodo, setNewTodo] = useState('');

  useEffect(() => {
    fetchTodos();
  }, []);
```

```
const fetchTodos = async () => {
  try {
    const response = await
fetch('http://localhost:5000/api/todos');
    const data = await response.json();
    setTodos(data);
  } catch (error) {
    console.error('Error fetching todos:', error);
  }
};

const handleAddTodo = async (e) => {
  e.preventDefault();
  try {
    const response = await
fetch('http://localhost:5000/api/todos', {
      method: 'POST',
      headers: {
        'Content-Type': 'application/json',
      },
      body: JSON.stringify({ text: newTodo }),
    });
    const data = await response.json();
    addTodo(data);
    setNewTodo('');
  } catch (error) {
    console.error('Error adding todo:', error);
  }
```

```
  };

  return (
    <div>
      <h1>Todo List</h1>
      <ul>
        {todos.map(todo => (
          <li key={todo.id}>{todo.text}</li>
        ))}
      </ul>
      <form onSubmit={handleAddTodo}>
        <input
          type="text"
          value={newTodo}
          onChange={(e) => setNewTodo(e.target.value)}
          placeholder="Add new todo"
        />
        <button type="submit">Add Todo</button>
      </form>
    </div>
  );
}

export default TodoList;
```

Both Redux and the Context API provide ways to manage global state in your application. Redux is more powerful and scalable, while the Context API is simpler and built into React.

Handling asynchronous operations

Asynchronous operations are a crucial part of web development. In React, we often use the `useEffect` hook to perform side effects like data fetching. For more complex async operations, we can use libraries like Redux Thunk or Redux Saga with Redux, or custom hooks with the Context API.

Here's an example using Redux Thunk:

```bash
npm install redux-thunk
```

```javascript
// store.js
import { configureStore, createSlice } from
'@reduxjs/toolkit';
import thunk from 'redux-thunk';

const todoSlice = createSlice({
  name: 'todos',
  initialState: { items: [], loading: false, error:
null },
  reducers: {
    fetchTodosStart: (state) => {
      state.loading = true;
    },
```

```
    fetchTodosSuccess: (state, action) => {
      state.items = action.payload;
      state.loading = false;
    },
    fetchTodosFailure: (state, action) => {
      state.error = action.payload;
      state.loading = false;
    },
    addTodoSuccess: (state, action) => {
      state.items.push(action.payload);
    },
  },
});

export const {
  fetchTodosStart,
  fetchTodosSuccess,
  fetchTodosFailure,
  addTodoSuccess
} = todoSlice.actions;

export const fetchTodos = () => async (dispatch) => {
  dispatch(fetchTodosStart());
  try {
    const response = await
fetch('http://localhost:5000/api/todos');
    const data = await response.json();
    dispatch(fetchTodosSuccess(data));
  } catch (error) {
```

```
    dispatch(fetchTodosFailure(error.message));
  }
};


export const addTodo = (text) => async (dispatch) => {
  try {
    const response = await
fetch('http://localhost:5000/api/todos', {
      method: 'POST',
      headers: {
        'Content-Type': 'application/json',
      },
      body: JSON.stringify({ text }),
    });
    const data = await response.json();
    dispatch(addTodoSuccess(data));
  } catch (error) {
    console.error('Error adding todo:', error);
  }
};


export const store = configureStore({
  reducer: {
    todos: todoSlice.reducer,
  },
  middleware: [thunk],
});
```

Real-time updates with WebSockets

WebSockets allow for real-time, bidirectional communication between the client and server. Let's implement real-time updates for our todo list using Socket.IO:

First, install Socket.IO on both the server and client:

```bash
npm install socket.io

npm install socket.io-client
```

Update the server:

```javascript
// server.js
const express = require('express');
const http = require('http');
const { Server } = require('socket.io');
const cors = require('cors');
const app = express();
const server = http.createServer(app);
const io = new Server(server, {
  cors: {
    origin: 'http://localhost:3000',
    methods: ['GET', 'POST'],
  },
```

```
});
app.use(cors());
app.use(express.json());
let todos = [
  { id: 1, text: 'Learn React', completed: false },
  { id: 2, text: 'Learn Node.js', completed: false }
];

io.on('connection', (socket) => {
  console.log('A user connected');
  socket.on('disconnect', () => {
    console.log('User disconnected');
  });

  socket.on('addTodo', (todo) => {
    const newTodo = { id: todos.length + 1, text: todo,
completed: false };
    todos.push(newTodo);
    io.emit('todoAdded', newTodo);
  });
});
app.get('/api/todos', (req, res) => {
  res.json(todos);
});
server.listen(5000, () => {
  console.log('Server running on port 5000');
});
```

Update the React component:

```jsx
// TodoList.js
import React, { useState, useEffect } from 'react';
import io from 'socket.io-client';
const socket = io('http://localhost:5000');
function TodoList() {
  const [todos, setTodos] = useState([]);
  const [newTodo, setNewTodo] = useState('');
  useEffect(() => {
    fetchTodos();
    socket.on('todoAdded', (todo) => {
      setTodos((prevTodos) => [...prevTodos, todo]);
    });
    return () => {
      socket.off('todoAdded');
    };
  }, []);

  const fetchTodos = async () => {
    try {
      const response = await
fetch('http://localhost:5000/api/todos');
      const data = await response.json();
      setTodos(data);
    } catch (error) {
      console.error('Error fetching todos:', error);
```

```
    }
  };

  const handleAddTodo = (e) => {
    e.preventDefault();
    socket.emit('addTodo', newTodo);
    setNewTodo('');
  };

  return (
    <div>
      <h1>Todo List</h1>
      <ul>
        {todos.map(todo => (
          <li key={todo.id}>{todo.text}</li>
        ))}
      </ul>
      <form onSubmit={handleAddTodo}>
        <input
          type="text"
          value={newTodo}
          onChange={(e) => setNewTodo(e.target.value)}
          placeholder="Add new todo"
        />
        <button type="submit">Add Todo</button>
      </form>
    </div>
  );
}
```

```
export default TodoList;
```

Now, when a todo is added, all connected clients will receive the update in real-time.

Testing full-stack applications

Testing is crucial for ensuring the reliability and maintainability of your application. Let's look at how to test both the frontend and backend of our todo application.

For the backend, we'll use Jest and Supertest:

```bash
npm install --save-dev jest supertest
```

```javascript
// server.test.js
const request = require('supertest');
const express = require('express');
const app = express();

// Import your routes
require('./server')(app);

describe('Todo API', () => {
  it('GET /api/todos --> array of todos', () => {
    return request(app)
```

```
    .get('/api/todos')
    .expect('Content-Type', /json/)
    .expect(200)
    .then((response) => {

expect(Array.isArray(response.body)).toBeTruthy();

expect(response.body.length).toBeGreaterThan(0);
      });
  });

  it('POST /api/todos --> created todo', () => {
    return request(app)
      .post('/api/todos')
      .send({
        text: 'Do something',
      })
      .expect('Content-Type', /json/)
      .expect(201)
      .then((response) => {
        expect(response.body).toHaveProperty('id');
        expect(response.body.text).toBe('Do
something');
      });
  });
});
```

For the frontend, we'll use Jest and React Testing Library:

```bash
npm install --save-dev @testing-library/react
@testing-library/jest-dom
```

```jsx
// TodoList.test.js
import React from 'react';
import { render, screen, fireEvent, waitFor } from
'@testing-library/react';
import '@testing-library/jest-dom/extend-expect';
import TodoList from './TodoList';
// Mock the fetch function
global.fetch = jest.fn(() =>
  Promise.resolve({
    json: () => Promise.resolve([{ id: 1, text: 'Test
todo', completed: false }]),
  })
);

describe('TodoList', () => {
  it('renders TodoList component', async () => {
    render(<TodoList />);

    expect(screen.getByText('Todo
List')).toBeInTheDocument();
```

```
    await waitFor(() => {
      expect(screen.getByText('Test
todo')).toBeInTheDocument();
    });
  });

  it('adds a new todo', async () => {
    render(<TodoList />);

    const input = screen.getByPlaceholderText('Add new
todo');
    const button = screen.getByText('Add Todo');
    fireEvent.change(input, { target: { value: 'New
todo' } });
    fireEvent.click(button);
    await waitFor(() => {
      expect(screen.getByText('New
todo')).toBeInTheDocument();
    });
  });
});
```

These tests cover basic functionality of both the backend API and the React frontend component. Remember to mock any external dependencies or API calls in your frontend tests to ensure they run consistently.

For end-to-end testing, you might consider using a tool like Cypress:

```bash
npm install --save-dev cypress
```

Create a new file `cypress/integration/todo_spec.js`:

```javascript
describe('Todo App', () => {
  it('adds a new todo', () => {
    cy.visit('http://localhost:3000');
    cy.get('input[placeholder="Add new
todo"]').type('New todo from Cypress');
    cy.get('button').contains('Add Todo').click();
    cy.contains('New todo from
Cypress').should('be.visible');
  });
});
```

This test visits your application, adds a new todo, and checks if it appears in the list.

To run Cypress tests, add a script to your `package.json`:

```json
```

```
"scripts": {
  "cypress:open": "cypress open"
}
```

Then run `npm run cypress:open` to open the Cypress Test Runner.

In conclusion, full-stack integration and data flow in a React and Node.js application involves several key aspects:

1. Connecting the frontend to the backend using HTTP requests (Fetch API or Axios).

2. Managing state with solutions like Redux or the Context API for more complex applications.

3. Handling asynchronous operations with hooks like useEffect or libraries like Redux Thunk.

4. Implementing real-time updates with WebSockets using libraries like Socket.IO.

5. Testing the full stack, including unit tests for the backend API, component tests for the React frontend, and end-to-end tests with tools like Cypress.

Remember that this is just a starting point. As your application grows, you might need to consider more advanced topics like:

- Authentication and authorization

- Error handling and logging

- Performance optimization

- Continuous Integration and Continuous Deployment (CI/CD)

- Containerization with Docker

- Serverless architecture

Always strive to keep your code modular, well-tested, and follow best practices for both React and Node.js development. Regularly update your dependencies and stay informed about the latest developments in the JavaScript ecosystem.

ADVANCED REACT TECHNIQUES

Server-side rendering with Next.js

Server-side rendering (SSR) is a technique that allows you to render React components on the server, which can improve initial load times and SEO. Next.js is a popular framework that makes SSR with React easy to implement.

Let's start by creating a new Next.js project:

```bash
bash

npx create-next-app my-nextjs-app
cd my-nextjs-app
```

Now, let's create a simple page with SSR:

```jsx
jsx

// pages/index.js
import { useState } from 'react';

export default function Home({ initialData }) {
  const [data, setData] = useState(initialData);


  return (
    <div>
      <h1>Welcome to Next.js!</h1>
```

```jsx
      <p>Server-side rendered data: {data}</p>
      <button onClick={() => setData(Math.random())}>
        Generate new data
      </button>
    </div>
  );
}
export async function getServerSideProps() {
  // This function runs on the server
  const initialData = Math.random();
  return { props: { initialData } };
}
```

In this example, `getServerSideProps` runs on the server for every request, generating some initial data. This data is then passed as props to the component, which can use it for the initial render.

Next.js also supports static site generation (SSG) for pages that can be pre-rendered at build time:

```jsx
// pages/static-page.js
export default function StaticPage({ buildTime }) {
  return (
    <div>
      <h1>Static Page</h1>
      <p>This page was built at: {buildTime}</p>
    </div>
  );
```

```
}
export async function getStaticProps() {
  return {
    props: {
      buildTime: new Date().toISOString(),
    },
    // Re-generate the page at most once per hour
    revalidate: 3600,
  };
}
```

This page will be generated at build time and can be served statically. The `revalidate` option enables Incremental Static Regeneration, allowing the page to be regenerated in the background as traffic comes in.

Code splitting and lazy loading

Code splitting is a technique that allows you to split your code into various bundles which can then be loaded on demand or in parallel. React.lazy provides a way to dynamically import components.

Here's an example:

```jsx
import React, { Suspense, lazy } from 'react';
const LazyComponent = lazy(() =>
import('./LazyComponent'));
```

```
function MyComponent() {
  return (
    <div>
      <h1>My Component</h1>
      <Suspense fallback={<div>Loading...</div>}>
        <LazyComponent />
      </Suspense>
    </div>
  );
}
```

In this example, `LazyComponent` will only be loaded when it's needed. The `Suspense` component provides a fallback UI to show while the lazy component is being loaded.

You can also use dynamic imports for code splitting without React.lazy:

```jsx
import React, { useState } from 'react';
function MyComponent() {
  const [module, setModule] = useState(null);
  const loadModule = () => {
    import('./heavyModule')
      .then(mod => setModule(mod.default))
      .catch(err => console.error('Failed to load
module', err));
  };
  return (
```

```jsx
    <div>
      <button onClick={loadModule}>Load Heavy
Module</button>
      {module && <module.Component />}
    </div>
  );
}
```

This approach gives you more control over when and how modules are loaded.

Custom hooks and reusable components

Custom hooks allow you to extract component logic into reusable functions. Here's an example of a custom hook for handling form input:

```jsx
jsx

import { useState } from 'react';
function useInput(initialValue) {
  const [value, setValue] = useState(initialValue);
  const handleChange = (event) => {
    setValue(event.target.value);
  };
  return {
    value,
    onChange: handleChange,
  };
}
```

```jsx
function Form() {
  const nameInput = useInput('');
  const emailInput = useInput('');
  const handleSubmit = (event) => {
    event.preventDefault();
    console.log('Submitted:', nameInput.value,
emailInput.value);
  };
  return (
    <form onSubmit={handleSubmit}>
      <input {...nameInput} placeholder="Name" />
      <input {...emailInput} placeholder="Email"
type="email" />
      <button type="submit">Submit</button>
    </form>
  );
}
```

This `useInput` hook encapsulates the logic for handling input state, making it easy to reuse across different form fields.

For reusable components, consider creating a component library. Here's a simple example of a reusable Button component:

```jsx
jsx

import React from 'react';
import PropTypes from 'prop-types';
import styles from './Button.module.css';
```

```jsx
function Button({ onClick, children, variant =
'primary', size = 'medium' }) {
  return (
    <button
      onClick={onClick}
      className={`${styles.button} ${styles[variant]}
${styles[size]}`}
    >
      {children}
    </button>
  );
}
Button.propTypes = {
  onClick: PropTypes.func.isRequired,
  children: PropTypes.node.isRequired,
  variant: PropTypes.oneOf(['primary', 'secondary',
'danger']),
  size: PropTypes.oneOf(['small', 'medium', 'large']),
};
export default Button;
```

This Button component is highly reusable and customizable. You
can use it like this:

```jsx
jsx

<Button onClick={() => console.log('Clicked')}
variant="secondary" size="large">
  Click me!
</Button>
```

Animations and transitions

React doesn't have built-in animation capabilities, but you can use CSS transitions or animation libraries like Framer Motion. Here's an example using CSS transitions:

```jsx
import React, { useState } from 'react';
import './Accordion.css';
function Accordion({ title, children }) {
  const [isOpen, setIsOpen] = useState(false);
  return (
    <div className="accordion">
      <button onClick={() => setIsOpen(!isOpen)}
className="accordion-title">
        {title}
      </button>
      <div className={`accordion-content ${isOpen ?
'open' : ''}`}>
        {children}
      </div>
    </div>
  );
}
```

```css
/* Accordion.css */
```

```css
.accordion-content {
  max-height: 0;
  overflow: hidden;
  transition: max-height 0.3s ease-out;
}
.accordion-content.open {
  max-height: 1000px; /* Adjust based on your content
*/
}
```

For more complex animations, you might want to use a library like Framer Motion:

```bash
npm install framer-motion
```

```jsx
import React from 'react';
import { motion } from 'framer-motion';
function AnimatedBox() {
  return (
    <motion.div
      initial={{ opacity: 0, scale: 0.5 }}
      animate={{ opacity: 1, scale: 1 }}
      transition={{ duration: 0.5 }}
      whileHover={{ scale: 1.1 }}
      whileTap={{ scale: 0.9 }}
```

```
    >
      Hover or tap me!
    </motion.div>
  );
}
```

This creates a div that animates in when it first appears, and responds to hover and tap interactions.

Internationalization and localization

For internationalization (i18n) and localization, you can use libraries like react-intl or react-i18next. Let's look at an example using react-i18next:

First, install the necessary packages:

```bash
npm install react-i18next i18next
```
"

Set up i18next:

```javascript
// i18n.js
import i18n from 'i18next';
import { initReactI18next } from 'react-i18next';

i18n
  .use(initReactI18next)
```

```
  .init({
    resources: {
      en: {
        translation: {
          "welcome": "Welcome to my app!",
          "language": "Language",
          "switch_language": "Switch Language"
        }
      },
      es: {
        translation: {
          "welcome": "¡Bienvenido a mi aplicación!",
          "language": "Idioma",
          "switch_language": "Cambiar Idioma"
        }
      }
    },
    lng: "en", // default language
    fallbackLng: "en",
    interpolation: {
      escapeValue: false
    }
  });

export default i18n;
```

Now, use it in your React components:

```jsx
import React from 'react';
import { useTranslation } from 'react-i18next';
import './i18n';
function App() {
  const { t, i18n } = useTranslation();
  const changeLanguage = (lng) => {
    i18n.changeLanguage(lng);
  };

  return (
    <div>
      <h1>{t('welcome')}</h1>
      <p>{t('language')}: {i18n.language}</p>
      <button onClick={() =>
changeLanguage('en')}>English</button>
      <button onClick={() =>
changeLanguage('es')}>Español</button>
    </div>
  );
}
export default App;
```

This setup allows you to easily switch between languages and translate your app's content.

For handling plural forms and complex translations, react-i18next provides additional features:

```javascript
javascript

// in your i18n config
{
  "key_one": "{{count}} item",
  "key_other": "{{count}} items",
  "complex": "{{what}} is {{how}}"
}

// in your component
t('key', { count: 1 }); // -> 1 item
t('key', { count: 5 }); // -> 5 items
t('complex', { what: 'i18next', how: 'great' }); // ->
i18next is great
```

These advanced React techniques can significantly improve the performance, user experience, and global reach of your applications. Here are some key takeaways:

1. Server-side rendering with Next.js can improve initial load times and SEO.

2. Code splitting and lazy loading can reduce initial bundle size and improve load times.

3. Custom hooks and reusable components can make your code more modular and easier to maintain.

4. Animations and transitions can greatly enhance user experience when used appropriately.

5. Internationalization and localization can help your app reach a global audience.

Remember, while these techniques are powerful, they should be applied judiciously. Always consider the specific needs of your project and your users when deciding which techniques to implement.

As you continue to develop your React skills, keep exploring new libraries and techniques. The React ecosystem is constantly evolving, and staying up-to-date with the latest best practices and tools can help you build better, more efficient applications.

SCALING AND OPTIMIZING NODEJS APPLICATIONS

Caching Strategies

Caching is a crucial technique for improving the performance of Node.js applications. It involves storing frequently accessed data in a fast-access storage layer to reduce the load on your database and speed up response times.

Let's look at a few caching strategies:

1. In-memory caching with Node.js

For simple applications, you can use an in-memory cache:

```javascript
const NodeCache = require('node-cache');
const myCache = new NodeCache({ stdTTL: 100,
checkperiod: 120 });

function getCachedData(key, fetchFunction) {
  const value = myCache.get(key);
  if (value) {
    return Promise.resolve(value);
  }

  return fetchFunction().then(result => {
    myCache.set(key, result);
```

```
      return result;
  });
}


// Usage
app.get('/api/data', (req, res) => {
  getCachedData('myKey', () => {
    // This function will only be called if the data
isn't in the cache
    return fetchDataFromDatabase();
  })
    .then(data => res.json(data))
    .catch(err => res.status(500).json({ error:
err.message }));
});
```

2. Redis for distributed caching

For distributed systems, Redis is a popular choice:

```javascript
const redis = require('redis');
const { promisify } = require('util');
const client = redis.createClient();
const getAsync = promisify(client.get).bind(client);
const setAsync = promisify(client.set).bind(client);

async function getCachedData(key, fetchFunction) {
  const cachedValue = await getAsync(key);
```

```javascript
  if (cachedValue) {
    return JSON.parse(cachedValue);
  }

  const result = await fetchFunction();
  await setAsync(key, JSON.stringify(result), 'EX',
3600); // Cache for 1 hour
  return result;
}

// Usage
app.get('/api/data', async (req, res) => {
  try {
    const data = await getCachedData('myKey',
fetchDataFromDatabase);
    res.json(data);
  } catch (err) {
    res.status(500).json({ error: err.message });
  }
});
```

3. Caching HTTP responses with `apicache`

For caching entire HTTP responses:

```javascript
javascript

const apicache = require('apicache');
const cache = apicache.middleware;
app.get('/api/data', cache('1 hour'), (req, res) => {
```

```javascript
// This handler will only be executed if the response
isn't cached
  fetchDataFromDatabase()
    .then(data => res.json(data))
    .catch(err => res.status(500).json({ error:
err.message }));
});
```

Load Balancing and Clustering

Node.js is single-threaded, but you can take advantage of multi-core systems using the built-in `cluster` module or PM2.

1. Using the `cluster` module:

```javascript
javascript

const cluster = require('cluster');
const http = require('http');
const numCPUs = require('os').cpus().length;
if (cluster.isMaster) {
  console.log(`Master ${process.pid} is running`);
  // Fork workers.
  for (let i = 0; i < numCPUs; i++) {
    cluster.fork();
  }

  cluster.on('exit', (worker, code, signal) => {
    console.log(`worker ${worker.process.pid} died`);
```

```
    cluster.fork(); // Replace the dead worker
  });
} else {
  // Workers can share any TCP connection
  // In this case it is an HTTP server
  http.createServer((req, res) => {
    res.writeHead(200);
    res.end('Hello World\n');
  }).listen(8000);
  console.log(`Worker ${process.pid} started`);
}
```

2. Using PM2:

First, install PM2 globally:

```bash
npm install -g pm2
```

Then, start your application with PM2:

```bash
pm2 start app.js -i max
```

This will start your app in cluster mode, using the maximum number of available CPU cores.

For load balancing across multiple servers, you can use a reverse proxy like Nginx:

```nginx
nginx

http {
    upstream myapp {
        server 192.168.0.1;
        server 192.168.0.2;
        server 192.168.0.3;
    }
    server {
        listen 80;
        location / {
            proxy_pass http://myapp;
        }
    }
}
```

Microservices Architecture

Microservices architecture involves breaking down your application into smaller, independently deployable services. Here's a simple example of how you might structure a microservices-based application:

1. API Gateway (app.js):

```javascript
javascript

const express = require('express');
const proxy = require('express-http-proxy');
const app = express();
app.use('/users', proxy('http://user-service:3000'));
```

```javascript
app.use('/products', proxy('http://product-
service:3001'));
app.use('/orders', proxy('http://order-service:3002'));
app.listen(80, () => console.log('API Gateway running
on port 80'));
```

2. User Service (user-service.js):

javascript

```javascript
const express = require('express');
const app = express();
app.get('/users', (req, res) => {
  // Fetch users from database
  res.json([{ id: 1, name: 'John Doe' }, { id: 2, name:
'Jane Doe' }]);
});
app.listen(3000, () => console.log('User service
running on port 3000'));
```

3. Product Service (product-service.js):

javascript

```javascript
const express = require('express');
const app = express();
app.get('/products', (req, res) => {
  // Fetch products from database
  res.json([{ id: 1, name: 'Widget', price: 9.99 }, {
id: 2, name: 'Gadget', price: 19.99 }]);
});
```

```javascript
app.listen(3001, () => console.log('Product service
running on port 3001'));
```

4. Order Service (order-service.js):

```javascript
javascript

const express = require('express');
const app = express();
app.post('/orders', (req, res) => {
  // Create a new order
  res.json({ message: 'Order created successfully' });
});
app.listen(3002, () => console.log('Order service
running on port 3002'));
```

Each of these services can be developed, deployed, and scaled independently.

Containerization with Docker

Docker allows you to package your application and its dependencies into a container, ensuring consistency across different environments.

Here's a sample Dockerfile for a Node.js application:

```dockerfile
"dockerfile

# Use an official Node runtime as the parent image

FROM node:14

# Set the working directory in the container to /app

WORKDIR /app

# Copy package.json and package-lock.json to the working directory

COPY package*.json ./

# Install any needed packages specified in package.json

RUN npm install

# Bundle app source inside the docker image

COPY . .
```

```
# Make port 8080 available to the world outside
this container

EXPOSE 8080

# Define the command to run your app using CMD
which defines your runtime

CMD [ "node", "app.js" ]
```
"

To build and run your Docker container:

```bash
docker build -t my-node-app .

docker run -p 8080:8080 my-node-app
```
"

For a multi-container application using Docker Compose:

```yaml
version: '3'

services:

  api-gateway:

    build: ./api-gateway

    ports:
```

```
      - "80:80"
  user-service:
    build: ./user-service
  product-service:
    build: ./product-service
  order-service:
    build: ./order-service
  redis:
    image: "redis:alpine"
"
```

Run this with:

```
"bash
docker-compose up
"
```

Deployment and CI/CD Pipelines

Continuous Integration and Continuous Deployment (CI/CD) automate the process of testing and deploying your application. Here's an example using GitHub Actions for a Node.js application:

```yaml
name: Node.js CI/CD
on:
  push:
    branches: [ main ]
  pull_request:
    branches: [ main ]
jobs:
  build:
    runs-on: ubuntu-latest
    steps:
    - uses: actions/checkout@v2
    - name: Use Node.js
      uses: actions/setup-node@v2
      with:
```

```yaml
      node-version: '14.x'
  - run: npm ci

  - run: npm run build --if-present

  - run: npm test
deploy:
  needs: build

  runs-on: ubuntu-latest

  if: github.ref == 'refs/heads/main'


  steps:
  - uses: actions/checkout@v2

  - name: Deploy to Heroku

    uses: akhileshns/heroku-deploy@v3.12.12

    with:

      heroku_api_key:
${{secrets.HEROKU_API_KEY}}

      heroku_app_name: "your-app-name"

      heroku_email: "your-email@example.com"
```

"

This workflow will run tests on every push and pull request, and deploy to Heroku when changes are pushed to the main branch.

When scaling and optimizing Node.js applications, keep these key points in mind:

1. Implement caching strategies to reduce database load and improve response times.

2. Use clustering or a process manager like PM2 to take advantage of multi-core systems.

3. Consider a microservices architecture for large, complex applications that need to scale independently.

4. Use containerization with Docker to ensure consistency across different environments and simplify deployment.

5. Implement a CI/CD pipeline to automate testing and deployment processes.

Here are some additional tips for optimizing Node.js applications:

1. Use asynchronous operations: Node.js is designed for non-blocking I/O operations. Always use asynchronous methods when dealing with I/O to prevent blocking the event loop.

```javascript
// Bad
const data = fs.readFileSync('/path/to/file');
processData(data);
```

```
// Good
fs.readFile('/path/to/file', (err, data) => {
  if (err) throw err;
  processData(data);
});
```

2. Implement proper error handling: Unhandled exceptions can crash your Node.js application. Use try-catch blocks and handle Promise rejections.

```javascript
process.on('uncaughtException', (err) => {
  console.error('Uncaught Exception:', err);
  // Perform cleanup if needed
  process.exit(1);
});
process.on('unhandledRejection', (reason, promise) => {
  console.error('Unhandled Rejection at:', promise,
'reason:', reason);
  // Perform cleanup if needed
});
```

3. Use streaming for large files: Instead of loading entire files into memory, use streams to process them in chunks.

```javascript
const fs = require('fs');
const zlib = require('zlib');
```

```javascript
fs.createReadStream('input.txt')
  .pipe(zlib.createGzip())
  .pipe(fs.createWriteStream('input.txt.gz'));
```

4. Profile your application: Use tools like `node --prof` or third-party profilers to identify performance bottlenecks in your code.

5. Optimize your database queries: Use indexes, limit the fields you're selecting, and use pagination for large result sets.

```javascript
// Instead of
const users = await User.find();
// Use
const users = await User.find().select('name
email').limit(10).skip(20);
```

6. Use connection pooling for databases: This helps in efficiently managing database connections.

```javascript
const mysql = require('mysql');
const pool  = mysql.createPool({
  connectionLimit : 10,
  host            : 'example.org',
  user            : 'bob',
  password        : 'secret',
  database        : 'my_db'
});
```

```javascript
pool.query('SELECT * FROM users', (error, results,
fields) => {
  if (error) throw error;
  console.log('The solution is: ', results);
});
```

7. Implement rate limiting to prevent abuse of your API:

```javascript
javascript

const rateLimit = require("express-rate-limit");
const apiLimiter = rateLimit({
  windowMs: 15 * 60 * 1000, // 15 minutes
  max: 100 // limit each IP to 100 requests per
windowMs
});
app.use("/api/", apiLimiter);
```

By implementing these strategies and continuously monitoring and optimizing your application, you can build scalable and efficient Node.js applications that can handle high loads and provide a great user experience.

Remember, optimization is an ongoing process. Regularly review your application's performance, stay updated with the latest Node.js features and best practices, and always profile before optimizing to ensure you're addressing the real bottlenecks in your application.

SECURITY BEST PRACTICES

HTTPS and SSL/TLS implementation

HTTPS (Hypertext Transfer Protocol Secure) is a secure version of HTTP that encrypts data transmitted between a client and a server. It uses SSL (Secure Sockets Layer) or its successor, TLS (Transport Layer Security), to provide this encryption.

Why HTTPS is crucial:

1. Data privacy: Encrypts sensitive information during transmission

2. Data integrity: Prevents data tampering

3. Authentication: Verifies the identity of the server

Implementing HTTPS in a Node.js application:

First, you'll need an SSL/TLS certificate. For testing, you can create a self-signed certificate using OpenSSL:

```bash
openssl req -nodes -new -x509 -keyout server.key -out server.cert
```

Now, let's create a simple HTTPS server:

```javascript
const https = require('https');
const fs = require('fs');
const express = require('express');
const app = express();
app.get('/', (req, res) => {
  res.send('Hello, secure world!');
});

const options = {
  key: fs.readFileSync('server.key'),
  cert: fs.readFileSync('server.cert')
};
https.createServer(options, app).listen(443, () => {
  console.log('HTTPS server running on port 443');
});
```

For production, you should use a certificate from a trusted Certificate Authority (CA) like Let's Encrypt.

To enforce HTTPS in an Express application, you can use the `helmet` middleware:

```javascript
const express = require('express');
const helmet = require('helmet');
const app = express();
```

```
app.use(helmet());
app.use(helmet.hsts({
  maxAge: 31536000,
  includeSubDomains: true,
  preload: true
}));
// Your routes here
```

This sets various HTTP headers to improve security, including Strict-Transport-Security (HSTS) which tells browsers to always use HTTPS for your site.

Cross-Site Scripting (XSS) prevention

Cross-Site Scripting (XSS) is a security vulnerability that allows attackers to inject malicious scripts into web pages viewed by other users.

Types of XSS

1. Stored XSS: Malicious script is stored on the server and served to users

2. Reflected XSS: Malicious script is embedded in a URL and executed when the URL is accessed

3. DOM-based XSS: Malicious script is executed by manipulating the DOM in the victim's browser

Preventing XSS

1. Input Validation and Sanitization:

Always validate and sanitize user input before using it in your application.

```javascript
const express = require('express');
const validator = require('validator');
const app = express();
app.use(express.json());
app.post('/user', (req, res) => {
  let username = req.body.username;
  if (!validator.isAlphanumeric(username)) {
    return res.status(400).json({ error: 'Invalid username' });
  }
  // Proceed with user creation
});
```

2. Output Encoding:

When displaying user-generated content, always encode it to prevent script execution.

In a React application:

```jsx
jsx

import React from 'react';
import DOMPurify from 'dompurify';

function UserContent({ content }) {
  return <div dangerouslySetInnerHTML={{__html:
DOMPurify.sanitize(content)}} />;
}
```

3. Content Security Policy (CSP):

Implement a strict Content Security Policy to control which resources can be loaded and executed.

In your Express application:

```javascript
javascript

const helmet = require('helmet');
app.use(helmet.contentSecurityPolicy({
  directives: {
    defaultSrc: ["'self'"],
    scriptSrc: ["'self'", "'unsafe-inline'", 'trusted-cdn.com'],
    styleSrc: ["'self'", 'trusted-cdn.com'],
    imgSrc: ["'self'", 'trusted-cdn.com', 'data:'],
    connectSrc: ["'self'", 'api.yourdomain.com'],
    fontSrc: ["'self'", 'fonts.gstatic.com'],
```

```
      objectSrc: ["'none'"],
      mediaSrc: ["'self'"],
      frameSrc: ["'none'"],
   },
}));
```

Cross-Site Request Forgery (CSRF) protection

CSRF is an attack that tricks the victim into submitting a malicious request to a website where they're authenticated. This can result in unauthorized actions performed on behalf of the authenticated user.

Preventing CSRF:

1. CSRF Tokens:

Generate and validate unique tokens for each form submission.

In an Express application using the `csurf` middleware:

```javascript
const express = require('express');
const csrf = require('csurf');
const cookieParser = require('cookie-parser');
const app = express();
app.use(cookieParser());
app.use(csrf({ cookie: true }));
app.get('/form', (req, res) => {
  res.send(`
    <form action="/submit" method="POST">
```

```
      <input type="hidden" name="_csrf"
value="${req.csrfToken()}">
      <input type="text" name="data">
      <button type="submit">Submit</button>
    </form>
  `);
});

app.post('/submit', (req, res) => {
  res.send('Data submitted successfully');
});
app.use((err, req, res, next) => {
  if (err.code !== 'EBADCSRFTOKEN') return next(err);
  res.status(403).send('CSRF token validation failed');
});
```

2. SameSite Cookies:

Set the `SameSite` attribute on cookies to restrict how they are sent with cross-site requests.

```javascript
app.use(session({
  secret: 'your-secret-key',
  cookie: {
    sameSite: 'strict',
    secure: true, // Ensure this is true when using
HTTPS
```

```
      httpOnly: true
   }
}));
```

3. Custom Headers:

For AJAX requests, you can require a custom header that simple HTML forms can't add.

```javascript
app.use((req, res, next) => {
   if (req.method === 'POST' && !req.headers['x-
requested-with']) {
      return res.status(403).json({ error: 'CSRF
validation failed' });
   }
   next();
});
```

On the client-side, ensure all AJAX requests include this header:

```javascript
fetch('/api/data', {
   method: 'POST',
   headers: {
      'Content-Type': 'application/json',
      'X-Requested-With': 'XMLHttpRequest'
   },
   body: JSON.stringify(data)
```

```javascript
});
```

API security and rate limiting

Securing your API is crucial to protect your application from abuse and unauthorized access.

1. Authentication and Authorization:

Implement robust authentication and authorization mechanisms.

Using JSON Web Tokens (JWT) for authentication:

```javascript
const express = require('express');
const jwt = require('jsonwebtoken');
const app = express();
const secretKey = 'your-secret-key';

app.post('/login', (req, res) => {
  // Validate user credentials
  const user = { id: 1, username: 'example' };
  const token = jwt.sign(user, secretKey, { expiresIn:
'1h' });
  res.json({ token });
});
function authenticateToken(req, res, next) {
  const authHeader = req.headers['authorization'];
  const token = authHeader && authHeader.split(' ')[1];
  if (token == null) return res.sendStatus(401);
```

```javascript
  jwt.verify(token, secretKey, (err, user) => {
    if (err) return res.sendStatus(403);
    req.user = user;
    next();
  });
}
app.get('/protected', authenticateToken, (req, res) =>
{
  res.json({ data: 'Protected resource' });
});
```

2. Rate Limiting:

Implement rate limiting to prevent abuse of your API.

Using the `express-rate-limit` middleware:

```javascript
javascript

const rateLimit = require('express-rate-limit');
const apiLimiter = rateLimit({
  windowMs: 15 * 60 * 1000, // 15 minutes
  max: 100 // Limit each IP to 100 requests per
windowMs
});


app.use('/api/', apiLimiter);
```

3. Input Validation:

Always validate and sanitize input data to prevent injection attacks.

Using `express-validator`:

```javascript
const { body, validationResult } = require('express-
validator');

app.post('/api/user',
  body('username').isAlphanumeric(),
  body('email').isEmail(),
  body('password').isLength({ min: 5 }),
  (req, res) => {
    const errors = validationResult(req);
    if (!errors.isEmpty()) {
      return res.status(400).json({ errors:
errors.array() });
    }
    // Process the request
  }
);
```

4. HTTPS:

Always use HTTPS for your API to encrypt data in transit.

5. API Versioning:

Implement API versioning to maintain backwards compatibility.

```javascript

app.use('/api/v1', v1Router);
app.use('/api/v2', v2Router);
```

Data encryption and secure storage

Protecting sensitive data at rest is as important as protecting it in transit.

1. Hashing Passwords:

Never store passwords in plain text. Always use a strong, slow hashing algorithm like bcrypt.

```javascript

const bcrypt = require('bcrypt');
async function hashPassword(password) {
  const saltRounds = 10;
  return await bcrypt.hash(password, saltRounds);
}
async function verifyPassword(password, hash) {
  return await bcrypt.compare(password, hash);
}
// Usage
app.post('/register', async (req, res) => {
  try {
    const hashedPassword = await
hashPassword(req.body.password);
    // Store hashedPassword in your database
```

```javascript
    res.status(201).send('User registered');
  } catch (error) {
    res.status(500).send('Error registering user');
  }
});
```

2. Encrypting Sensitive Data:

For data that needs to be decrypted later, use strong encryption algorithms.

```javascript
const crypto = require('crypto');
const algorithm = 'aes-256-cbc';
const key = crypto.randomBytes(32);
const iv = crypto.randomBytes(16);
function encrypt(text) {
  let cipher = crypto.createCipheriv(algorithm,
Buffer.from(key), iv);
  let encrypted = cipher.update(text);
  encrypted = Buffer.concat([encrypted,
cipher.final()]);
  return { iv: iv.toString('hex'), encryptedData:
encrypted.toString('hex') };
}

function decrypt(text) {
  let iv = Buffer.from(text.iv, 'hex');
```

```javascript
  let encryptedText = Buffer.from(text.encryptedData,
'hex');
  let decipher = crypto.createDecipheriv(algorithm,
Buffer.from(key), iv);
  let decrypted = decipher.update(encryptedText);
  decrypted = Buffer.concat([decrypted,
decipher.final()]);
  return decrypted.toString();
}

// Usage
const sensitiveData = "Secret message";
const encrypted = encrypt(sensitiveData);
console.log(encrypted);
const decrypted = decrypt(encrypted);
console.log(decrypted); // 'Secret message'
```

3. Secure Key Management:

Store encryption keys securely, preferably using a key management service.

4. Database Encryption:

Consider using database-level encryption for an additional layer of security.

For MongoDB, you can use field-level encryption:

```javascript
const mongoose = require('mongoose');
const encrypt = require('mongoose-encryption');
const userSchema = new mongoose.Schema({
  username: String,
  password: String,
  email: String,
  creditCard: String
});

const encKey = process.env.SOME_32BYTE_BASE64_STRING;
const sigKey = process.env.SOME_64BYTE_BASE64_STRING;

userSchema.plugin(encrypt, {
  encryptionKey: encKey,
  signingKey: sigKey,
  encryptedFields: ['creditCard']
});

const User = mongoose.model('User', userSchema);
```

5. Secure Configuration Management:

Never hardcode sensitive information like API keys or database credentials in your code.

Use environment variables:

```javascript
require('dotenv').config();
const dbConnection = mysql.createConnection({
  host: process.env.DB_HOST,
  user: process.env.DB_USER,
  password: process.env.DB_PASSWORD,
  database: process.env.DB_NAME
});
```

Store these in a `.env` file, which should be added to your `.gitignore`:

```
"DB_HOST=localhost

DB_USER=myuser

DB_PASSWORD=mypassword

DB_NAME=mydatabase

"
```

6. Regular Security Audits:

Regularly review and update your security measures. Use tools like npm audit to check for vulnerabilities in your dependencies.

```bash
"bash

npm audit"
```

7. Principle of Least Privilege:

Always follow the principle of least privilege. Only give users and processes the minimum level of access they need to perform their functions.

Remember, security is an ongoing process. Stay informed about the latest security threats and best practices, and regularly update and patch your systems.

Implementing these security measures will significantly enhance the safety of your web application. However, security is a complex and ever-evolving field. It's crucial to stay updated with the latest security trends and to regularly audit and update your security measures.

For particularly sensitive applications or those handling valuable data, consider hiring a professional security auditor or penetration tester to identify potential vulnerabilities in your system.

Lastly, remember that no system is ever 100% secure. The goal is to make it as difficult as possible for attackers to compromise your system, and to have robust monitoring and incident response plans in place to quickly detect and respond to any security breaches that do occur.

BUILDING MODERN WEB APPLICATIONS WITH REACT AND NODEJS

As we've explored throughout this guide, React and Node.js form a powerful combination for building modern, efficient, and scalable web applications. Let's recap the key aspects and benefits of this stack:

1. Frontend Development with React

React has revolutionized frontend development with its component-based architecture and virtual DOM. It allows developers to create reusable UI components, leading to more maintainable and efficient code. React's declarative nature makes it easier to understand and debug, while its robust ecosystem provides solutions for common development challenges.

Key takeaways:

- Component-based architecture promotes reusability and maintainability

- Virtual DOM enhances performance by minimizing actual DOM manipulations

- JSX syntax allows for intuitive integration of HTML-like code within JavaScript

- Rich ecosystem with libraries like React Router for navigation and Redux for state management

2. Backend Development with Node.js

Node.js enables JavaScript to run on the server-side, allowing for full-stack JavaScript development. Its event-driven, non-blocking I/O model makes it particularly well-suited for building scalable network applications.

Key takeaways:

- JavaScript on both frontend and backend reduces context switching for developers

- NPM (Node Package Manager) provides access to a vast library of open-source packages

- Asynchronous nature allows for efficient handling of concurrent operations

- Express.js framework simplifies the creation of robust API endpoints

3. Full-Stack Integration

The combination of React and Node.js allows for seamless integration between frontend and backend, facilitating the development of full-stack JavaScript applications.

Key takeaways:

- Shared language (JavaScript) between frontend and backend

- Easy data exchange using JSON

- Real-time capabilities with WebSockets for live updates

- Isomorphic/Universal JavaScript applications possible for improved SEO and initial load times

4. Performance and Scalability

Both React and Node.js are designed with performance in mind. React's virtual DOM minimizes costly DOM operations, while Node.js's non-blocking I/O allows it to handle many concurrent connections efficiently.

Key takeaways:

- React's efficient update mechanism ensures smooth user interfaces

- Node.js's event loop enables handling of multiple concurrent operations

- Microservices architecture can be easily implemented for further scalability

5. Developer Experience and Productivity

The React and Node.js ecosystem provides a range of tools and libraries that enhance developer productivity. From Create React

App for quick project setup to hot reloading for instant feedback during development, these tools streamline the development process.

Key takeaways:

- Rich set of development tools and debugging utilities

- Large and active community providing support and continuous improvements

- Extensive documentation and learning resources available

6. Security Considerations

As with any web application, security is a crucial aspect when building with React and Node.js. We've covered various security best practices, including:

- HTTPS implementation for secure data transmission

- Protection against common vulnerabilities like XSS and CSRF

- API security measures including authentication, authorization, and rate limiting

- Secure data storage and encryption practices

7. Future-Proofing Your Applications

The React and Node.js ecosystem is constantly evolving, with new features and improvements being regularly introduced. Staying updated with the latest versions and best practices ensures that your applications remain modern and efficient.

Key takeaways:

- Regular updates to both React and Node.js introduce performance improvements and new features

- Growing ecosystem continuously provides new tools and libraries to solve emerging challenges

- Strong community support ensures longevity and relevance of both technologies

In conclusion, the combination of React for frontend development and Node.js for backend services provides a robust, efficient, and scalable solution for building modern web applications. This stack allows developers to leverage their JavaScript skills across the entire application, leading to faster development cycles and more consistent codebases.

The component-based architecture of React promotes code reusability and maintainability, while Node.js's event-driven model allows for building high-performance, scalable backend services. Together, they enable the creation of everything from simple single-page applications to complex, data-intensive web platforms.

However, it's important to remember that while React and Node.js provide powerful tools, they are just that - tools. The key to building successful web applications lies in understanding fundamental web development principles, following best practices, and continually learning and adapting to new technologies and methodologies.

As you continue your journey in web development with React and Node.js, remember to prioritize user experience, maintain clean and efficient code, and always keep security at the forefront of your development process. Stay curious, keep learning, and happy coding!

A Quick Favor Before You Go

If this book helped your learning journey, I'd appreciate you taking a moment to leave an honest review where you purchased this book. Reviews help the book reach the right readers and support future updates and improvements.

Thank you for ready.

— *Joseph Elmer*